bullshit. How to interact with people that suck. How to recognize and respect my boundaries and the boundaries of others. How to be grateful for badass companies and colleagues.

I've also had shitty bosses (not naming names, but the literal crackhead may have been the standout on this list) and amazing ones (Hi, Pam! Hi, M'Joyce! And hi Larry who is now managing his own company and hiring my board interns, giving a whole new generation of counselors a great employment experience!). And I gained just as many skills from both the amazing ones AND the shitty ones. We gain "what not to do" skills in the same way that we gain "what to do" skills.

And I've noticed this comes up a lot. With my aforementioned board interns. And with my clients.

While they aren't coming in for career counseling per se, dealing with work bullshittery impacts all areas of life. If work sucks, you end up carrying that shit home with you way more than you want to. And so we talk about how to handle it. And there are common themes in all of these conversations. And I realized that practical conversations about handling this stuff don't really happen.

I used to teach Career Counseling to graduate students. We focused on theory, assessment, job placement strategies, working with individuals that needed supported employment. All the stuff they needed to pass the state licensing exam to become counselors after graduation. But no pragmatics about just plain ol' *working*. The day to day not losing your mind at work part of life. Which is the far BIGGER part of life, when you think about it.

So I started taking notes about what came up the most, and the conversations and strategies that seemed to help people manage. And this list was the final result.

1) **The world doesn't revolve around you.** I would like to say that's because it clearly revolves around me, but sadly that isn't the case either. One of my aforementioned great bosses (the fabulous Pam) told me that one day. I was supremely butthurt about something that escapes me now, and was pretty sure everyone was colluding to make my life miserable. She called me on that bullshit, and she was right.

   Generally speaking? You aren't really registering on people's radar nearly as much as you'd think. If people are shitty, it's because THEY are shitty. Or the system y'all are operating in is shitty. Not because they have it out for you. Probably like 95% of the time it's about them, or the system, or other externals.

   That's important to understand because it will help you to better recognize, respond, and be respected when you complain about the 5% of the time when it actually IS about you.

2) **The number of people who have a say in determining your self-worth should probably only be counted on about one hand.**

   I worked with someone a few years ago who was objectively heinous. Like seriously nasty. If you met her on the street she would likely glare at your or roll her eyes to the heavens this is her default setting and you would think *"What the fuck is her malfunction?"*

I was walking into a local bar and saw several of my colleagues drowning their sorrows over the meeting we had that afternoon with Mistress Heinous. I was on my way to meet a date. They invited me to commiserate but I passed, saying I was fine (plus, the date). One person asked me "But she was so horrible to you, how come you aren't affected by her?"

Well, for a few reasons. She's horrible to everyone, therefore it wasn't about me (see above). And in terms of our jobs, we worked together just fine (see below) but most importantly? **She had zero effect on my self-worth.** This is not just a job lesson, this is a life lesson. There are very few people who know me and love me well enough that if they were shitty to me it would really hurt. And it would hurt because it meant something was seriously wrong between us. My list is a pretty small list and yours probably should be as well. And if a colleague or supervisor is on it, it should only be because they are also a mentor who is equally invested in their relationship with you.

This doesn't mean that you shouldn't feel bad if you genuinely upset someone and their upset-ness is well deserved. You should apologize authentically, rectify whatever you can, and don't do the shitty thing again to the best of your ability. Own your fuck-ups. But even then their upset-ness isn't something you should carry around as a soul wound. This shouldn't smash you in the solar plexus. And if this upset person has an upset-ness that has zero to do with your actions? *Then this doesn't need to be carried by you at all.* Figure out who is on your list, and remind yourself of this when people NOT on the list are getting to you.

3) **You don't have to be besties, you just have to be able to work together. For that matter, they can suck balls at their job as long as their behavior isn't affecting your ability to do YOUR job.**

So the aforementioned heinous, nasty, horrible bitch? Was damn good at her job. (Which was why she still had one, TBH.) If we were on a project together, shit got done. Other than having the personality of a rusty razorblade, working with her was not a problem. And she respected my WORK, even when she didn't respect my PERSONHOOD. And I'd rather deal with an effective asshole, than a nice moron any day.

Even harder for me, but even more freeing was when I finally ceased to give a shit about people being shitty at their jobs as long as they weren't impeding mine. Because it got to be exhausting, resenting all the fucktards that were making the same amount of money as me (or, usually, more) while going around being fucktards. My general philosophy ever since has been "be helpful or move outta my way" and it sure made things more tolerable. Just imagine yourself putting these people in the corner with a juice box and some crayons. They can color while the adults are working. Other people's incompetence isn't your problem, unless you are their supervisor, in which case you already have the power to do something about it. If it's really affecting your ability to do *your* job, that's the time you need to have a convo with their actual supervisor. Otherwise it's their problem and not yours.

4) Tattle on yourself. It makes life easier.

"Jesus Christ, Harper, I never even get a chance to catch you doing something stupid…you always catch yourself first and confess."

No matter what my role, whether an employee or a supervisor, I always confessed my sins right away. Sure, I could wait to see if I got caught. Chances are I wouldn't, right? And if I was the boss? Just let that shit ride out, no worries. First of all, being sneaky is dick behavior (and if you read my *Adulting* zine, you know how I feel about being a dick). No matter what role you are in, if you are honest about when you mess up, everyone around you will trust you. And you can function far more effectively if everyone around you trusts you. Unless they are batshit crazy, supervisors will be far less likely to micromanage you and far more likely to give you extra growth opportunities within the company if you operate from a place of honesty.

And if you are a supervisor? Owning your bullshit, taking responsibility, and apologizing will buy you more devotion from your employees than a bad-ass salary and a basket of muffins. If you step in with a *"That was my call, she was acting on my authority, so this conversation should be between us, not you and her"* or you say *"That didn't work, and I really appreciate everyone trying to make it work. Let's look at new options, what do y'all think?"* then people will know that (a) you aren't trying to be a dick, (b) you aren't gonna throw them under the bus, (c) you actually give a shit about them and their work, and (d) you really are trying to do a good job.

5) Praise the fuck out of awesomeness and give credit where it's due.

Some years ago, I was working as a quality assurance administrator. An epically thankless job in many ways. I was auditing clinical notes (because, ugh) and happened to read a few that were really great. I sent a quick email to that staff member, telling them that their documentation was great, and the quality of their work with their clients really shone through, and I appreciated them, and that it made my job really great at that moment. This wasn't a required thing. Generally we looked for problems. The reports I filled out were only "Plan of Improvement" forms. So, if there was no problem, it didn't show up. Makes sense, right?

This particular person emailed me back, and told me they had been so frustrated and felt so unsupported that they had printed out their 2 week notice that same day, and had planned on giving it to their supervisor at the end of the week. But my email kept them from doing so. We would have lost someone AMAZING just because we had all failed to verbalize how amazing she really was. And you better believe that my "Plan of Improvement" forms started becoming full of superlatives after that. Full of "no improvement needed, great note!" or "I loved this, this, and this… we only need to work on this" instead of a laundry list of negs.

I made sure it came up in meetings, along with great ideas in general. I would say "so and so had a great idea and gave me permission to steal it and use it" when presenting a new plan. Again, this is also stuff that makes your trustworthiness apparent, and your desire to be supportive crystal clear. The little things make all the difference…sometimes literally between staying and leaving.

6) Ask without presuming intent. And give people the out.

I complained to my literal-crackhead boss about not being told about a meeting I should have been at. Her response: *"Well, it wasn't INTENTIONAL, calm down!"* Twenty years later, I'm still pretty damn sure it was intentional, but that's beside the point. The actual point is that I looked like an asshole and a drama queen and she looked like the aggrieved party dealing with a princess employee. Bad move. One of my interns asked me recently how to approach her boss about a similar move. I have a far better way of dealing with such shenanigans after that experience. I stay strictly factual and even give people all benefit of the doubt.

Can you imagine the better response I would have gotten not just from the crackhead, but from the person who was both our administrator if I had said *"Hey, I didn't see we had a manager's meeting today. I figure either you were slammed and forgot to let me know or you knew I was slammed and were trying to cut me a break, but I know it's a meeting that is important for me to be at. Is at a certain regular time so I can add it to my calendar, or do I need to make sure I get on the invite list?"* So if someone wasn't being intentionally shitty, you weren't just presuming they were. And even if they were, you just make an uncomfortable conversation far more bearable while still insuring that that bullshit ain't happening a second time without serious fallout. I've used it dozens of times over the years after I learned my lesson, and it hasn't failed me yet.

7) Ask for what you want in specifics. Have the data to back it up.

As someone who has been both the ask-er and the ask-ee, I can tell you that you will have far more success if you are very specific, to the point, and you have data available to prove your point. There is nothing more frustrating than needing something pretty basic to be successful at your job and being told "NEIN", right? And true story, some people are going to be total dick-faces no matter what you ask for…like a bathroom break and a 3-cent raise will make you uniquely responsible for the downfall of Western civilization.

But that doesn't mean it isn't worth asking, and you might be surprised by what you are able to get. I've had jobs where it was my responsibility to squeeze money from a stone, and I was pretty good at it because I would do my research, create a budget breakdown, and even demonstrated where the money could be sourced…from elsewhere in the budget or pimping and ho-ing as the case may be (or as we call it in community mental health, accessing external funding streams through grant writing and corporate sponsorship). Some true-from-my-life examples:

1) I was working with teen moms with children under the age of three. All of the teen moms in our program needed to learn infant

CPR and first aid. I researched how much the instructor class cost and all the mannequins I would then need to teach the moms. I reached out to a company that was new in town and could use a little feel-good PR and asked them to pay for it. I looked into how we could give them same-said PR (a meet and greet with your local mayor thanking them for supporting a local, valuable program) and presented the whole thing to my supervisor as a fait accompli. If I had just said "we really need to find a way to teach all the moms infant CPR and first aid" nothing would have happened. And within the first 6 months of starting the program, one 18-month old's life was saved by their trained mom. My boss wasn't an asshole who wanted babies to die, but she was overworked and we were underfunded and people came to her all the time with these kinds of problems. I presented the solution WITH the problem.

2) My boss at a community agency was bitching about how slow the crisis assessors were. Rather than just think they were stupid and lazy, I followed them around for a bit and realized they had to fill out every form on paper with the client, then bring it back to their desktop and enter it all online. Yeah, that'll slow you down. I talked to people doing similar work at hospitals and other agencies, and they got laptops put on wheelie-carts with wireless so they could get online. So clearly, we needed the same. Tell my boss we needed some bankage for new tech?

Good luck. Instead I went straight to our IT division to find out what our IT budget was. Turns out they were due for new desktops in the next 6 months, so I was able to go in with the proposal that we reallocate that money to COWs (computers on wheels). So I wasn't able to resolve the issue immediately, but she knew WHAT the problem was, and we were able to correct it within a year by not continuing to spend the money we DID have I stupid ways.

3) Of course, not every problem has a monetary solution. Letting people be who they are is absolutely FREE, after all. You wouldn't think respecting people's names and pronouns would be such a difficult fucking task with mental health providers. Our jobs are supposed to be healthy identity formation, right? But I have fought at more than one place about respecting names and pronouns of trans* and gender-nonconforming folx. You would think that saying *"fundamental human fucking RIGHTS"* would be enough, but nope. I still live in Texas and had to change the nature of the argument. So I started presenting the issue in a different, less emotional, more pragmatic way. Yes, legal name goes in the billing strip. But if we would refer to "William" as "Billy" (or Junior, or Dude, or insert middle name or nickname here), we can absolutely refer to "William" as "Bettina" if that's her name. While I love to throw down over deadnaming/intentional misgendering,

that wasn't the fight we were having in this case. They were worried about their billing and reimbursement, and didn't care one bit about the intricacies of the singular "they." So when I showed them that the billing wouldn't be rejected, the fight was over.

It may not be something tangible, though. You may want to get new opportunities that will help build your resume and experience within an organization. Two different people I used to work with approached me, asking for opportunities to do some training within our organization. Both came in with information about their past experience, their specific interests, and their future goals. I hooked them both up, and both of them leapfrogged into supervisory roles within other companies in a couple of years. They had hustle and asked for opportunity and mentoring. And now I have contacts in two new places... it's a win-win for a good manager. Find your person and approach them like the organized, ass-busting superhero you are.

8) Don't ask people to do work you aren't willing to do and don't ask people to work harder than you are working.

Wanna be the go-to person? Be the motherfucker that shuts it *down*. Produce whatever needs to be produced. Whether you are a supervisor or not, you can still lead by example. No one ever busted my chops about bathroom cleaning or dish washing duty when I was managing a sandwich shop because I was in the same rotation for the shit jobs. And even as a colleague working at the same level, I would almost always get support from my coworkers because I was out there busting my ass as hard as I could. It takes a special kind of asshole to not up their game when you've upped yours. Yeah, I know those they exist, but most people rise to the occasion, if only because you just publically shamed them into doing so.

Also? It's easy to get frustrated with how it seems that everyone gets jobs or moves up in their workplace anymore. And if you are reading this, you likely aren't the boss's kid, therefore are not one of those people with a leg up to move up. And when that's the case it's easy to think you have no fucks in your pocket because you can't compete at that level. But if you DON'T have a Daddy Moneybags to hook you up, the only thing you DO have is your ability to kick ass. I've always preferred the person who worked hard and was eager to learn than the person who was wicked-smart and thought that everything going on was beneath them.

9) Remember your supporting role.

This is how you find the pony in the pile of shit. Yes, you may be working for a place whose ultimate concern is profit and it's real fucking easy to feel like you sold your soul to Satan. And your employer may, empirically, be either Satan or one of her high-ranking minions. My husband will wax poetic about the fact that if you run a business that is incorporated in the United States, it is actually your *legal obligation* to make money. He will then spend another 15 minutes espousing why this is the fundamental problem with the world today. I tend to think the fundamental problem with the world today is that my favorite bakery stopped carrying my favorite cookie. But he's probably more correct than I am.

True Story O'Clock:

Back to managing a sandwich shop. The patriarch of the family who owned the string of shops, pulled us all in one day to yell. They had broken down what their profit was per sandwich. It was six cents. Now bear in mind, that was pure profit that did not include all the nice salaries EVERYFUCKINGFAMILYMEMBER was drawing from the business. This was the profit OVER how much everyone was getting paid to be "managers" or "district managers" or whatever-the-fuck titles they had that sometimes got in the way of working on their tennis game.

Patriarch had also broken down what each napkin cost. Yeah, seriously. He was out for blood and looking for any reason to bitch. He then told us that when we grabbed a whole handful of napkins to give to the customer instead of the "one napkin for a 6 inch or two for a footlong" we were **STABBING HIM THROUGH THE HEART.** As creative as I am I could not make this shit up.

And this is soul-deadening bullshittery to its core. And the kind of thing that will eat you alive if you let it.

So me being who I am, I continued to give out extra napkins when people asked for them. Because mustard and mayonnaise are as messy as fuck, amirite? And despite my continuous heart-stabbing behavior, I was promoted into management. Because my store made money when the other stores were not. But my store wasn't turning profit because of my excellent napkin wrangling skills.

My store made money because my focus was on taking care of people who were coming in for lunch or dinner and making that a nice experience for them. I gave them extras…a little extra tuna on their sub, extra napkins, an extra cookie. I remembered what the pregnant lady was craving, and we joked about how her kid would come in ordering the same sandwich in future years.

I refused to make my job about making money for the Napkin Police, but instead made it about supporting *people*. And then the money making took care of itself.

> Because I was not just the person who made them their sandwich (they could go to several other places for that), I was the person who cared about their lives. I was their *friend* at the sandwich shop.
>
> When I left that company because I got my first job in the mental health profession, they freaked out. Hardcore. This was before cellphones and stuff, so they found out where I was working (a town a couple hours away) and started calling the business. I would get dragged up to the main office to answer their calls. They begged me to come back. They offered me any of the stores in the chain if I didn't want to come back to mine. They offered me a district manager position. The calls lasted for months…because they started losing money (as well as the staff that had worked for me) when they went back to a napkin-counting way of managing a business.

I carried that with me throughout my career. <u>Who am I here to support?</u> If I am providing a direct service, I'm supporting the people I provide the service to. If I am a supervisor, I am supporting the people who are providing services. That is my job…PERIOD. And the money making part has *always taken care of itself* when I do that.

10) Do the best you can, as often as you can, for as long as you can. Until you can't.

You are not going to feel 100% every day you clock in. As much as I love my job, there are plenty of days I'd rather curl up in bed with a book or three and a cat or three. But if I'm committed to showing up, I'm not going to do a half-assed job of it. My clients, interns, students, and team members deserve the best me. (It probably also helps that one of my businesses is a publishing house I co-founded with my husband. So if I do a shitty job, he can find me pretty easily)

This sounds simple, but there may become a point where it isn't doable anymore. Your job sucks so bad, you can't find what you need inside yourself to do the best you can anymore.

And you have to be really aware of your internal signals that that's the case. Are you going through a year's worth of sick days in three months? Do you feel nausea and dread the evening before you have to go into work? Do you feel that you can't find a way to connect to your supporting role anymore? Do the people who know you best keep asking what your *malfunction* is?

It would be awesome to be able to torch bridges on our way out the door the minute that happens. This isn't an actual feasible option 99.44% of the time, as you well know. But start to plan your escape route. Even if you have to dig out that wall for years on end like you are Tim Robbins in The Shawshank Redemption, you will find being there far more tolerable every day that you're digging.

My husband was recently chatting with a guy in a shitty job where he was being epically bullied. He had talked to a lawyer about the case, who said he wanted 10K up front to handle the case.

My husband told him the case was likely a loser if this was what the lawyer was saying, but said he'd check with me (as someone who knows federal bullying laws pretty damn well).

I agreed. The bullying wasn't attached to circumstances that were federally protected (religion, ethnicity, etc.). The case couldn't be won. The guy wanted another job but couldn't find one that paid nearly as well. It sucked all the time.

The company he worked for, however, has a great program for paying for additional schooling. My suggestion was go back to school on their dime for something he was really interested in doing, that would give him a ton more freedom in the future (in this case, nurse practitioner). He is still digging away at that prison wall, but after he crawls through those miles and years of shit, he's going to finally achieve freedom.

In the meantime, he doesn't feel so powerless. He does all that he can do, then he goes to night classes on the company dime.

His supporting role worldview has shifted back to *himself* and he is able to get through his days with his soul intact.

And when you do leave, don't take a crap (literally or metaphorically) on your boss's desk on your way out the door (even if this practice constitutes my husband's sole suggestion for this zine). Even if you know there is no fuckingbloodyhell way you would ever work there again, you can be honest about why you are leaving without stooping to their toolbox level while doing so.

The kinds of things to say:

1) I had many good experiences working there, but ultimately, I found that many of the things I was hoping to accomplish didn't mesh with the goals or the organization.
2) I think the organization is in a rebuilding phase right now and will be in a really good place in the future. I worked with some amazing people, and I know they will continue to do amazing things there.
3) I left for very specific reasons (they included, XYZ). These reasons are about me, not about the company in it's entirety or everyone that works there.

And I promise you, people will *get it.* They will totally know what you are saying (especially if you work for a place that's well known for their dickitude) and future employers will love the fact that you don't shit-talk former employers. When I drop one of those lines, usually people laugh and say "Gotcha. Thanks." And we move on, both understanding what was left unsaid.

And you may find yourself bumping up against those former employers again, and having left gracefully may pay off in spades. (I've actually done contract work for companies I have left. It allowed me to effect real change when being an employee there did not. And I could do that because I never trashed them publicly when we both knew I could have.) It has also allowed me the Plan Z of going back to work there if I ever needed a job on the quick. My reputation with them was intact, and sometimes the job market dictates having to eat a little crow in order to keep a roof over your head.

So that's it. Dr Faith's working advice. All taken from decade of fucking up and learning lessons the hard way. And from knowing that no one fucking talks about any of this in a useful and pragmatic way. In a job market that is changing weirdly and wildly and at a crazy-rapid pace, we all need all the help we can get. And I'm well aware that most of us have no interest in working for a company for 20 years and then taking retirement and a gold watch the way our grandparents did. If those jobs even exist anymore, TBH. Chances are, you're like me and you want to get off the hamster wheel, and create a career where you work for yourself and have control over whatever you put out in the world. So the question is…does this working shit still matter if it's not my endgame?

Hell, yeah. Striking out on my own successfully was due in large part to my reputation when working for others. People talk. Even big cities are tiny as fuck when it comes to workplace gossip. These are your contacts for the rest of your days. You want them to be your biggest fans.